DATE

Government Wage-Price Guideposts
in the American Economy

THE CHARLES C. MOSKOWITZ LECTURES   NUMBER VII

GEORGE MEANY

PRESIDENT
AMERICAN FEDERATION OF LABOR AND
CONGRESS OF INDUSTRIAL ORGANIZATIONS

ROGER M. BLOUGH

CHAIRMAN OF THE BOARD
AND CHIEF EXECUTIVE OFFICER
UNITED STATES STEEL CORPORATION

NEIL H. JACOBY

DEAN
GRADUATE SCHOOL OF BUSINESS ADMINISTRATION,
UNIVERSITY OF CALIFORNIA AT LOS ANGELES

Government Wage-Price Guideposts

in the American Economy

THE CHARLES C. MOSKOWITZ LECTURES
SCHOOL OF COMMERCE   1967
NEW YORK UNIVERSITY

SINCE THE PUBLICATION of the *Economic Report of the President* in January, 1962, an important topic of economic discussion has been the productivity-based wage-price guideline policy which it introduced. That this should be so is no occasion for surprise, considering the importance of the national economic objectives which underlay its adoption; namely, (1) the achievement of full employment, interpreted as meaning a 96 per cent employment rate, at least as an initial target; (2) simultaneously with the accomplishment of the employment goal, the avoidance of an upward inflationary thrust in the price level; and (3) as an adjunct of price level stability, the attainment of major improvement in our balance-of-payments position. Of course, the specific question which was central was: Can the government stimulate aggregate effective demand sufficiently, through appropriate monetary and fiscal policies, to achieve a 96

per cent employment rate without simultaneously stimulating an inflationary thrust in the price level and further
endangering an already serious balance-of-payments
situation?

The question was sharpened by the knowledge that
the price level had moved up most markedly in those
postwar years when the employment rate was 95 per
cent or more, and the unemployment rate 5 per cent or
less. In fact, years in which the employment rate varied
between 93 and 95 per cent were characterized by
moderate or little movement in both the Consumer Price
Index and the Wholesale Price Index. Since the Kennedy
and Johnson administrations considered an employment
rate between 93 and 95 per cent inadequate and wished
to stimulate the economy to achieve a 96 per cent or
higher rate, the inflationary potential of the employment
target was a real and immediate concern.

The analysis of the Council of Economic Advisers
led them to conclude that general price level increases,
associated with a decline in the employment rate from
5 per cent to 4 per cent, reflected the exercise of market
power by strong business and labor groups, rather than
being a result of excess aggregate demand and "tight"
product and labor markets. Given this conclusion, the
productivity-based wage-price guideline policy, backed
by the weight of federal influence, exercised directly and
indirectly, coupled with an informed public opinion, was
thought to be a sufficiently strong counterpoise to private
economic power to check inflation while the economy
expanded. In the language of the Council:

While rising prices will not necessarily accompany the expansion we expect in 1962, neither can we rely on chance to keep our price level stable. Creeping inflation in the years 1955–57 weakened our international competitive position. We cannot afford to allow a repetition of that experience.

We do not foresee in 1962 a level of demand for goods and services which will strain the economy's capacity to produce . . .

But in those sectors where both companies and unions possess substantial market power, the interplay of price and wage decisions could set off a movement toward a higher price level. If this were to occur, the whole nation would be the victim.

❋   ❋   ❋   ❋   ❋   ❋   ❋   ❋   ❋   ❋   ❋

The Nation must rely on the good sense and public spirit of our business and labor leaders to hold the line on the price level in 1962. If labor leaders in our major industries will accept the productivity benchmark as a guide to wage objectives, and if management in these industries will practice equivalent restraint in their price decisions, the year ahead will be a brilliant chapter in the record of the responsible exercise of freedom.[1]

Thus, the wage-price guideline policy was born. Made more rigid in the January 1964 *Economic Report of the President,* it continued to be the announced policy of the government through 1966. However, in 1966 it was buffeted mercilessly. Indeed, it was shattered in a number of important and widely publicized collective

---

1 *Economic Report of the President, January 1962,* (Washington: U.S. Government Printing Office), pp. 16–17.

bargaining settlements, that is, the New York City transit strike settlement, the airlines agreement, and so on. In this context, the 1966 Charles C. Moskowitz lecture series of the School of Commerce of New York University was devoted to a discussion of "Government Wage-Price Guideposts in the American Economy." The Moskowitz Lectures, established through the generosity of Charles C. Moskowitz, a distinguished alumnus of the School of Commerce and formerly Vice President, Treasurer, and a Director of Loew's, Inc., have enabled the School to make a significant contribution to public discussion and understanding of important issues affecting the American economy and its business enterprises.

The 1966 lecture series was fortunate in the combination of speakers it was able to present. Outstanding in their qualifications, they brought to the platform an extraordinary aggregate of experience in labor, business, education and public service. Thus, it was with a substantial sense of satisfaction that the lectures were introduced. The opening lecture brought to our audience the views of Mr. George Meany, President of the American Federation of Labor and Congress of Industrial Organizations, on "Wage and Price Policies and Trends." The second lecture was delivered by Mr. Roger M. Blough, Chairman of the Board and Chief Executive Officer of the United States Steel Corporation. He discussed "Guideposts—A Business View OR Can Good Economics be Good Politics?" The final speaker was Dr. Neil H. Jacoby, Dean of the Graduate School of Business at the University of California, and a former member of the Council of Economic Advisers. He spoke on "Wage-

Price Guideposts and Alternative Instruments to Attain United States Economic Goals."

Although the Council of Economic Advisers and some university economists, like Professor Robert M. Solow of the Massachusetts Institute of Technology, strongly supported the guidepost policy, an opposite consensus was expressed by the Moskowitz lecturers. But their agreement did not extend beyond a common disbelief in the effectiveness and economic soundness of the guidepost policy.

Mr. Meany began his lecture by observing that the market power of labor was neither so great nor so influential on prices as was that of major corporations, seeming to imply thereby that the guidepost policy was in error in viewing both groups equally. Beyond this point, the major thrust of his address concerned the distribution of income in the nation. According to Mr. Meany, the economic expansion of the period 1961–66 was disproportionately favorable to capital and profits, with labor and wages lagging behind in benefits. As a consequence, he feared an increasing lack of balance between the economy's power to produce and its capacity to spend for consumption, with, in turn, an impairment of long-run economic growth without sharp cyclical movements. With this view of the economic situation, Mr. Meany expressed the belief that the effect of the guidepost policy was to unduly limit wage increases, while consumer prices and corporate profits continued to rise and more than swallowed the benefits of increased productivity. He maintained, in addition, that the guidepost policy was unsatisfactory because:

(1) no single productivity figure could be applied to the enormously varied individual wage-setting situations arising in the economy every year; (2) trade unions and collective bargaining procedures involve less than a majority of America's wage and salary earners; and (3) the minority which is involved is represented by a number of autonomous national and international unions which negotiate an aggregate of some 150,000 different bargaining agreements, so that the United States does not have the highly centralized labor and employer institutions which might be able to make a guidepost policy work. In conclusion, Mr. Meany indicated that organized labor would support even-handed restraint on all costs, including prices and profits as well as wages and salaries, in the event the nation's economic viability warranted the adoption of extraordinary stabilization methods.

Where Mr. Meany saw corporate power as a critical element underlying upward price movements, Mr. Blough discerned the source of difficulty as the "unique statutory power of organized labor." Beyond labor's power, Mr. Blough saw the context of the full employment objective and the government's commitment to it—a commitment born of the economic catastrophe of the 1930s and kept alive by a haunting memory of it. However, governmental pursuit of full employment is associated with inflation, so that a dilemma confronts policy makers; that is, full employment with inflation, or price level stability with less than full employment. Mr. Blough observed that "Confronted by this dilemma, it was natural that government should temporize—as governments historically have—by trying to restrain rising prices without

materially lessening the expansionary economic policies
which were a fundamental cause of the problem. And
so . . . , the wage-price guideposts made their
debut . . ." Having focused on the policy dilemma
which produced the guidepost approach, Mr. Blough
reviewed its evolution observing that since 1962 the
guideposts had become more rigid in computation and
more compulsory in application. Appraising them in this
frame of reference, his conclusion was negative, although
he did feel they had some virtue in focusing public attention on the relationship among wages, productivity, and
prices. Essentially, Mr. Blough pointed to these shortcomings: (1) the ineffectiveness of the wage guideposts
as a check on wage increases, while government applied
the price guidepost successfully in such highly visible
industries as steel, copper, etc.; (2) the diversity of the
economy, so that a single productivity trend figure was
unsuitable and should not be applied to many specific
cases; (3) the fact that productivity advances resulted
from non-labor inputs which must be compensated, so
that the entire productivity gain was not available for
wage increases; (4) the belief that the wage guidepost
tended to undermine individual initiative, impaired the
political security of labor leaders, and interfered with
the normal flow of labor from job to job; and (5) the
belief that the price guidepost was irreparably flawed
because it ignored and defied "the immutable law of
supply and demand," and the price decisions which are
ultimately determined in the market place. All in all,
Mr. Blough saw the guidepost policy as being in a state
of suspended animation in the autumn of 1966. But his

expressed hope was that, in its place, the political leaders
of the nation would face the underlying truths about inflation and full employment and would inform the
public about them, so that the time would come in our
country "when good economics becomes good politics"
and "the age-old problem of inflation" would "be laid to
rest without the loss of human freedom."

Although agreeing that the guideposts had become
ineffective during 1966, Dean Jacoby seemed more concerned with this question: "Are there better ways to
resolve the problem of attaining full employment and
rapid growth without price inflation in a market-directed
economy?" To arrive at an answer, he reviewed the basic
theory of the quideposts, traced their evolution into a
major policy tool, sought to define "full employment" and
"price level stability" in operationally useful terms, and
assessed the magnitude of the problem involved in their
reconciliation. In this process of analysis, Dean Jacoby
made the important point that, while a 4 per cent unemployment rate was operationally useful as a full employment goal, *a complete lack* of upward movement in the
Consumer Price Index was not a reasonable definition of
price-level stability. To the contrary, an upward drift in
the CPI of *no more than* 1.5 per cent per year was viewed
by him as representing a non-inflationary price level.
He based this judgment on: (1) an upward bias in the
Index, due to technical procedures in its construction,
that is, tardy recognition of new products and quality
improvements; and (2) the historical record between
1958 and 1963, which showed an upward drift in the
CPI of less than 1.5 per cent per year without any

tendency toward acceleration. Given a full employment
goal of 96 per cent and a definition of price level stability
which allows up to 1.5 per cent rise in the CPI per year,
what public policies offer promise of simultaneously
achieving them? Dean Jacoby proposed this six-point
program: (1) broaden and enforce the antitrust laws,
with *all* private organizations which seek economic ends
being covered; (2) reduce the barriers to foreign trade
and widen the area of competition; (3) accelerate programs to retrain and relocate workers; (4) gradually
withdraw from governmental price-fixing and price-
supporting activities; (5) defer increases in the minimum
wage and extensions in its coverage; and (6) expand
research into labor market functioning, with the aim of
improving its efficiency. Finding the guideposts of some
use as a means of educating the public in wage-price-
productivity relationships, Dean Jacoby concluded that
they became detrimental when used as a system of
federally enforced wage and price controls. In his view,
"the basic means of reconciling full employment with a
stable price level is to restore effective competition in
all sectors of the U.S. economy." And to this end he put
forward his six-point program.

I would be remiss indeed if I did not express the
deep appreciation of the School of Commerce, as well as
my own, to Mr. Charles C. Moskowitz, supporter of the
lecture series, to Mr. George Meany, Mr. Roger M.
Blough, and Dean Neil H. Jacoby, the speakers, who
shared their knowledge and experience with us, and to
Mrs. Patricia Matthias, my administrative assistant, whose
editorial tenacity and attention to the technical details

associated with a smoothly-run program, made the lecture series pleasant as well as informative, and led finally to the publication of the papers.

Abraham L. Gitlow,
DEAN
SCHOOL OF COMMERCE
NEW YORK UNIVERSITY

February, 1967

THE CHARLES C. MOSKOWITZ LECTURES

THE MOSKOWITZ LECTURES have been established through the generosity of a distinguished alumnus of the School of Commerce, Mr. Charles C. Moskowitz of the Class of 1914, who retired after many years as Vice President-Treasurer and a Director of Loew's, Inc.

In establishing these lectures it was Mr. Moskowitz' aim to contribute to an understanding of the function of business and its underlying disciplines in society by providing a public forum for the dissemination of enlightened business theories and practices.

The School of Commerce and New York University are deeply grateful to Mr. Moskowitz for his continued interest in and contribution to the educational and public service program of his Alma Mater.

This volume is the seventh in the Moskowitz series. The earlier ones were:

Senior Economist,
J. Walter Thompson Company
Gilbert E. Jones, President,
IBM World Trade Corporation
Darrell B. Lucas, Professor of
Marketing and Chairman of the
Department, New York University

CONTENTS

WAGE AND PRICE POLICIES
AND TRENDS

by George Meany

PRESIDENT
AMERICAN FEDERATION OF LABOR AND
CONGRESS OF INDUSTRIAL ORGANIZATIONS

AT THE OUTSET, before getting into the detailed subject matter of this lecture, I think it is essential to underscore some basic principles that are all too often forgotten.

First, collective bargaining between free trade unions and employers is an integral part of American society. It provides workers, through their representatives, with a voice in the determination of their wages, hours of work, and working conditions. It establishes procedures for the orderly settlement of disputes at the work-place. It provides a major part of the machinery, in a free society, whereby workers can attempt to achieve a fair share of the fruits of the economy's progress.

With all of its imperfections and human mistakes, collective bargaining has continued to reveal its flexibility and adaptability to the rapid changes that are taking place in the thousands of different industries, markets, and occupations. These achievements have been made with a minimum of strife; about 98 per cent of collective bargaining negotiations have been concluded peacefully in recent years, and work-stoppages have accounted for less than two-tenths of one per cent of available work-time.

Secondly, wages and salaries are not merely a cost to employers and a factor in the price of goods and services. They are also income to workers and the major source of consumer buying power.

Emphasis on the cost-side of this issue, to the exclusion of the income-side, represents a lack of objectivity, as well as a disregard for the need of a growing, mass consumption base for the national economy. Any objective view must include consideration of both sides of this issue—wages are both income to workers and a cost to employers.

Moreover, the wages and salaries of employees are not the only costs to business. There are many other costs —such as the salaries, bonuses, expense accounts, and stock options of executives; the costs of raw materials, depreciation write-offs, interest payments on loans, and many other costs, as well as taxes. In addition, there are profits and dividends to stockholders.

Third, there are built-in restraints in the setting of wages that are not present in other economic factors.

In companies whose employees are not represented by trade unions, wages and salaries are set unilaterally by the employer. Where employees are represented by unions, wages and salaries are determined through the process of collective bargaining with the employer—and with the effective restraint of employer resistance.

In addition, millions of employees are covered by long-term agreements that require extensive periods of time before they are subject to renegotiation. Even short-term collective bargaining contracts "lock-in" the agreement's provisions for a year.

What is more, the reopening or renegotiation of collective bargaining contracts usually requires advance notice to the employer sixty to ninety days before the expiration date of the contract or its reopening. Frequently, the union states its demands before the negotiations begin. As a result, the union provides advance notice—available to the public and the government, as well as the employer—of its desire to change the terms of a collective bargaining contract.

Where prices are concerned, however, equal restraints do not exist. In several key industries, prices are set by the top executives of the dominant corporations—to provide high profit-returns on investment. The other companies in such industries usually follow along, rather rapidly, with the change in price.

In many other industries, prices respond quickly to immediate market opportunities—to what the traffic will bear.

Wage determination, then, is subject to employer resistance and to the time-lags and advance notice that are part of the collective bargaining process, as well as to the influence of economic conditions. Price-setting, on the other hand, has no such built-in restraints, except for the influence of changes in economic conditions. Moreover, in several key industries, the major corporations so dominate their industries that they set prices, with little, if any, effective price competition.

With these brief comments on a few basic principles, I will turn to an examination of trends and policies.

Wage Trends In Recent Years

The economic advance of recent years has brought benefits to the vast majority of Americans; but the distribution of these benefits among different groups in the population has been lopsided. Most of the fruits of the economic advance, to date, have gone to business.

Workers' wage gains have been rather modest in recent years. This is indicated by the figures reported by the Department of Labor.

Table 1

AVERAGE HOURLY EARNINGS *

	Manufac- turing	Contract Con- struction	Wholesale Trade	Mining
1965	$2.61	$3.69	$2.61	$2.92
1960	2.26	3.08	2.24	2.60
Average Yearly Rise	2.9%	3.7%	3.1%	2.3%
Sept. 1966	$2.74	$3.96	$2.75	$3.10
Sept. 1965	2.63	3.75	2.62	2.93
	4.2%	5.6%	5%	5.8%

* Includes the effect of overtime
Source: U.S. Department of Labor

Much of the buying power value of these gains in hourly earnings, however, was washed out by the rise of living costs—a yearly rise of 1.3 per cent in 1960–65 and a 3½ per cent increase between September 1965 and September 1966. Actual improvements in buying power were only about one-third to one-half of the gains in cents-per-hour.

Table 2

YEARLY INCREASES IN BUYING POWER
OF AVERAGE HOURLY EARNINGS

	Manufac- turing	Contract Con- struction	Wholesale Trade	Mining
1960–1965	1.6%	2.4%	1.8%	1.0%
Sept. 1965– Sept. 1966	0.7%	2.1%	1.5%	2.3%

Source: U.S. Department of Labor

Even after accounting for improvements in non-payroll fringe benefits—such as pension and health plans—the gains in real compensation per hour, since 1960, have been considerably less than 3 per cent a year. Yearly gains in the buying power of compensation per hour—including fringe benefits—were about 2.1 per cent for factory workers and 2.9 per cent for construction workers in 1960–65, and approximately 1.2 per cent for factory workers and 2.6 per cent for construction workers between September 1965 and September 1966.

These large groups of workers—and other similar groups, as well—did not receive a fair share of the country's rising prosperity.

The real volume of output per manhour, in the entire private economy, rose at an average yearly rate of about 3.6 per cent in 1960–65, according to the Department of Labor. But real compensation per hour of all employees in the private economy, including executives and supervisors, increased only about 2.6 per cent a year.

This trend reveals one measure of the degree to which wage and salary earners have been shortchanged in recent years—with the major share of the economy's forward advance going to profits, dividends and other types of property-income.

The slow rise of workers' buying power can be seen most clearly by examining the after-tax weekly take-home pay of wage and salary earners, after adjustment for rising living costs. Despite the increase in the number of hours worked per week in recent years—and the spread of overtime—gains in the buying power of take-home pay were modest between 1960 and 1965. And, in the past year, there has been practically no improvement at all in the buying power of take-home pay of large groups of workers.

This record reveals the modest progress of workers' buying power in a period of expanding economic activity. The vast majority of wage and salary earners have not shared equitably in the benefits of the national economy's growth. Moreover, the failure of workers' buying power to advance in the past year threatens to undermine the needed expansion of consumer markets

Table 3

THE BUYING POWER OF
WEEKLY TAKE-HOME PAY *
(Workers with Three Dependents)

	Manu-facturing	Contract Con-struction	Mining
1965	$88.06	$111.48	$100.34
1960	77.70	96.17	90.13
	$10.36	$ 15.31	$ 10.21
Average Yearly Rise	+2.5%	+3.0%	+2.2%
July–Sept. 1966	$87.34	$114.94	$101.72
July–Sept. 1965	87.54	113.34	100.84
	−.20	$ 1.60	$ .88
Percentage Rise	0	+0.1%	+0.1%

* Weekly earnings, after taxes, in constant dollars of 1957–59 buying power.
Source: U.S. Department of Labor

by falling short of the economy's increasing ability to produce more goods and services, more efficiently.

Changes In Costs and Prices

The price level has been rising, in recent years, despite the remarkable stability of unit labor costs (the costs of labor in each item produced). As President Johnson declared in his Economic Report of January

1966: "Labor costs—the most basic element in the structure of our costs—have barely moved, as gains in productivity have largely offset moderate increases in hourly labor costs."

In the entire private economy, unit labor costs increased merely about 3 per cent in 1960–65—an average yearly rise of approximately one-half of one per cent. But the cost of living rose more than twice as much —6.6 per cent in 1960–65, or an average yearly increase of 1.3 per cent.

This trend is continuing. In the year between September 1965 and September 1966, the cost of living jumped 3½ per cent. But it is clear that this rise of living costs is greater than the rise of unit labor costs in the entire private economy.

In the key manufacturing sector of the economy, unit labor costs actually declined 1.6 per cent between 1960 and 1965, according to the Department of Commerce. But the level of wholesale prices of manufactured goods rose 1.7 per cent—almost as much as the drop in unit labor costs.

Thus far in 1966, unit labor costs of manufactured goods increased somewhat, partly as a result of increased employer contributions to social security and partly due to workers' attempts to catch up with rising living costs. In the first nine months of 1966, these unit labor costs were about 1.5 per cent greater than in the same period of 1965. But wholesale prices of maunfactured goods rose 2.8 per cent.

As a result of these trends, the spread between prices and unit labor costs has been growing. In mid-1966, the spread between unit labor costs in manufacturing industries and the wholesale prices of manufactured products was greater than at any time since 1951, according to the Department of Commerce.

Table 4

THE GROWING SPREAD BETWEEN UNIT LABOR COSTS AND WHOLESALE PRICES OF MANUFACTURED GOODS

	Unit Labor Costs Mfg. Industries (1957–59 = 100)	Wholesale Prices Mfd. Goods (1957–59 = 100)	Ratio of Prices of Mfd. Goods to Unit Labor Costs (1957–59 = 100)
1960	100.6	101.1	100.4
1961	100.3	100.7	100.4
1962	100.4	100.8	100.3
1963	99.7	100.6	100.9
1964	99.7	101.1	101.4
1965	99.0	102.8	103.9
1st 9 mos. of 1965	98.8	102.6	103.8
1st 9 mos. of 1966	100.3	105.5	105.2

Source: U.S. Department of Commerce

Part of this large spread between unit labor costs and prices is due to increased prices of raw materials, sharply rising interest rates and similar factors. But most of this spread reflects increased profit margins on each item of goods that is sold.

These widened profit margins—accompanied by an expanding volume of sales—explain the skyrocketing profits of recent years.

Workers' Income and Business Income

The record reveals that profits have moved out of line with every other major type of income. Between 1960 and 1965, profits rose 52 per cent before taxes and 67 per cent after taxes and dividend payments to stockholders increased 43 per cent.

In contrast, the weekly after-tax take-home pay of factory workers increased only 21 per cent, merely 13 per cent after accounting for the rise of living costs. Total wages, salaries, and fringe benefits of all employees in the economy increased only 33 per cent—reflecting increased employment, as well as advances in wages and salaries. And total after-tax personal income in the entire economy increased 34 per cent.

The lack of balance continues in 1966. Between the first nine months of 1965 and the same period of 1966, profits rose about 10.5 per cent, both before and after taxes, and dividend payments to stockholders increased another 12 per cent, according to the U.S. Department of Commerce.

But the after-tax weekly take-home pay of factory workers increased only 2.8 per cent in that period, with almost no improvement in buying power. Total wages, salaries and fringe benefits of all employees increased

Table 5

THE LACK OF ECONOMIC BALANCE
1960–1965

Corporate Profits After Taxes	Up 66.7%
Corporate Profits Before Taxes	Up 52.3%
Dividend Payments to Stockholders	Up 43.3%
Factory Workers' Weekly Take-Home Pay	Up 20.8%
Total Wages, Salaries, Fringe Benefits of All Employees in the Economy	Up 33.3%
Total After-Tax Personal Income in the Economy	Up 34%

Source: U.S. Departments of Commerce and Labor

9.7 per cent. And total after-tax personal income in the entire economy rose only 8 per cent.

As a result of these contrasting trends, the wage and salary earners' share of the value of national production has been going down, while the business share has been increasing.

According to government reports, the after-tax rate of return of manufacturing corporations rose from 9.2 per cent of net worth in 1960 to 13 per cent of a substantially greater net worth in 1965 and 13.9 per cent in the first half of 1966. At the rate of return of 1965 and the first half of 1966—and with the addition of increasing depreciation write-offs—the average manufacturing corporation can recapture the value of its investment in approximately 4½ years.

Moreover, the corporate cash-flow, after tax payments, rose from $17.30 per $100 of corporate production in 1960 to $19.80 per $100 of output in 1965 and to nearly $20 in the first half of 1966. This corporate take-out of production is greater than in any year since 1950 —even greater than in 1955, which was a very good business year.

Inequities in income distribution have been developing and widening. These trends have been creating the basis for a lack of balance between the economy's increasing ability to produce more efficiently, and the slower rise in buying power of workers and consumers generally. Consumer markets are the base of the American economic system, and increasing real wages are essential for growing consumer markets.

Raises in real wages are needed to provide workers with a fair share of the fruits of the economy's progress. Justice and equity, as well as economic good sense, require increases in buying power. High business profits and the economy's increasing productive efficiency make possible such increases in wages and sales, without raising the price level. In fact, the profits and productivity of many companies are so great that they could simultaneously raise wages and cut their prices.

Wage and Price Policies

Actual wage and price decisions, of course, will be made within the context of the specific realities in the various markets that make up the American economy.

The U.S. is a huge country of continental size. There are tens of thousands of different markets, industries, and occupations. In each of them, there are a large number of specific and different conditions, a multitude of tangible factors, and real problems that have to be met.

For example, in a number of industries, there are wage inequities. In some industries or companies, there are substandard wages. In many industries, technological changes are displacing jobs, changing job content and skill requirements, and shifting job classifications, wage rates, and lines of promotion or downgrading; and the cost of living is rising, eating into workers' buying power. These issues are real and tangible to both workers and employers, and they require workable solutions.

For these reasons, no one single "magic number" can be imposed as the precise limit for all increases in hourly compensation of all employees throughout the varying and different markets, industries, and occupations. Moreover, an attempt to base such a single "magic number" on one economic factor alone—such as productivity—makes the idea even more unworkable. Productivity figures are not precise; at best, they are estimates. In addition, they are subject to frequent revision. I do not believe that any such single figure can be appropriately applied to the wages and salaries of millions of workers, who are confronted by varying conditions in their different places of work.

The structure of the American economy also makes such a "magic number" guideline unworkable. Actual decisions affecting wages and salaries are made either unilaterally by tens of thousands of different employers or through collective bargaining, between a multitude of national and local unions, on one side, and tens of thousands of employers and employer associations, on the other side.

There is no single national employers' association that can set the wages to be paid by all employers or even the vast majority of employers and also set the prices for all of their various products. Neither are there even a half-dozen centralized employers' associations that can determine the wages and prices for most companies.

On the employee side, only a minority of wage and salary earners are represented by trade unions. And for this organized group of employees, there is no single, national collective bargaining representative. The AFL-CIO is a federation of 128 autonomous national and international trade unions; it has no authority to bargain with employers on behalf of the members of its affiliated national and international unions.

As a result of the pluralistic and decentralized nature of American society, wage determination, too, is decentralized. There are about 150,000 different collective bargaining agreements between tens of thousands of employers and over one hundred national unions and their 70,000 local unions. Moreover, even where there are master agreements covering the employees of multi-plant corporations, there usually are supplemental plant agreements affecting wages, salaries, fringe benefits, seniority, and other issues.

It is for these and similar reasons that the AFL-CIO declared the so-called wage and price guidelines of the Council of Economic Advisers—with its precise "magic number" for wages—to be inequitable, largely one-sided, and unworkable. Moreover, there has been no effective price restraint policy to accompany the rather precise wage restraint policy and no profit restraint policy at all.

The statement adopted by the President's Advisory Committee on Labor-Management Policy on August 18, 1966, attempts to avoid such pitfalls. In my judgment, this statement points towards the possibility of a more workable framework for public policy.

The statement declares that "it is impractical if not impossible to translate the goals reflected in the guideposts into formulae for application to every particular price or wage decision. We believe that in a free society any policy to achieve price stability will be acceptable and effective only if it bears equitably on all forms of income."

The mechanism, recommended by the President's Labor-Management Committee, to seek the goals of rising real incomes and relative price stability, is along the following lines.

> In the near future and at least once a quarter thereafter an objective evaluation should be made of the economy by the Council of Economic Advisers to determine the extent to which the economy as a whole is achieving the goals reflected in the guideposts. . . . If the evaluation indicates that the overall economy is falling short of the goals reflected in the guideposts, the following steps be taken:
>
> 1   The Council of Economic Advisers should identify the nature and apparent chief causes of the major problems or shortcomings.
>
> 2   To the extent that the causes may relate to matters within the purview of the President's Advi-

sory Committee on Labor-Management Policy, representatives of that Committee and the Council of
Economic Advisers should discuss those problems
to determine whether any appropriate corrective
action can be recommended.

3   The President's Advisory Committee on Labor-
Management Policy should submit to the President
a report identifying the problems or shortcomings
and including recommendations for corrective action.

It is too early to know how this pragmatic approach
will work out, but it is based on a recognition that there
is a wide variety of different conditions among the
thousands of industries, markets, and occupations.

If the President determines that there is a national
emergency to warrant extraordinary stabilization measures—with even-handed restraints on all costs, prices,
profits, dividends, corporate executive compensation, as
well as employees' wages and salaries—he will have the
support of the AFL-CIO. We, of organized labor, are
prepared to sacrifice—as much as anyone else, for as long
as anyone else—so long as there is equality of sacrifice.

GUIDEPOSTS—A BUSINESS VIEW, *OR* CAN GOOD ECONOMICS BE GOOD POLITICS?

by Roger M. Blough

CHAIRMAN OF THE BOARD
AND CHIEF EXECUTIVE OFFICER
UNITED STATES STEEL CORPORATION

WHEN ARTHUR KROCK, veteran columnist of *The New York Times*, retired a few weeks ago after more than 33 years of continuous service in Washington, he wrote a "farewell column" appraising the national scene as he viewed it. And commenting on the current economic situation, he said:

> Price inflation is still being attacked on the flank, for the practical political reason that to strike at it frontally would require legislative curbs on the unique statutory power of the administration's political ally—organized labor—to raise the costs of production virtually at will.
>
> A frontal attack on inflation, would also require a meaningful reduction in government spending for non-military projects. . . . But this reduction would be opposed by another powerful ally of the Administration, the group whose goal is the total

21

welfare state to which the President's grandiose design of the Great Society is both kith and kin.

Now I quote this perceptive paragraph from Mr. Krock, not as my scriptural text for the day, but rather because it brings into penetrating focus the fact that any meaningful analysis of the government wage-price guideposts must give full weight to the political factors involved in dealing with inflation, and cannot, realistically, be confined to a discussion merely of their economic effects.

In many lands, in many centuries, many governments have grappled with the problem of inflation and have always found themselves impaled upon the horns of the same, inevitable, dilemma: that no politically palatable solution has been economically effective, while no economically effective solution has been politically palatable. This raises the question of whether good economics can be good politics—and vice versa.

It may also raise in your minds the question of why I have been honored with this opportunity to discuss the wage-price guideposts with you here today. Since I am neither an economist nor a politician, I am obviously at the somewhat happy disadvantage of being unable to speak with any pretense of authority. At the same time, however, I do have a somewhat unhappy advantage in that I have had certain close—and occasionally painful —contacts with the guideposts as they have operated and can, therefore, speak with the voice of experience and a modicum of feeling. And from this experience, let me add, has come a feeling of deep sympathy for the government official who must try to satisfy the economic desires of the electorate. Everyone wants prosperity and full employment. Twenty million elderly people want increased Social Security benefits, seventy-eight million members of the work force want ever-higher wages, and 115 million adult consumers do *not* want higher prices.

To pursue the political blessings of full employment, while avoiding the economic scourge of inflation, is to provide the best of all worlds for everyone. It is, at once, a politician's dream and an economist's nightmare, and it is out of this nocturnal restlessness that the guideposts were born.

Origins

If we seek the origins of these guideposts, we must look, I believe, to the seeds that were planted in the great depression of the 1930s when 25 per cent of the nation's work force was unemployed and when great numbers of people were destitute. There were soup kitchens and bread lines; and shanty-towns sprang up—often on city dumps where the homeless could find cast-off materials out of which to build shelters of a sort.

Confronted by these stark realities, a new administration in Washington decided to use boldly the enormous economic powers which lay at its command. Under the Constitution, government had the exclusive power to coin and regulate the value of money; it had the unrestricted power to tax and to borrow; and thus it had the un-limited power to spend. And it used them all in a deliberate effort to create inflation—although to call it that would not have been good politics. So officials spoke of "reflation" instead; but the difference was purely semantic.

As agencies emerged in alphabetical profusion, the WPA, the PWA, and one of the CCC's spent billions to create so-called "make-work" jobs. The AAA and the other CCC poured additional billions into the support of farm prices. The gold standard was abandoned, and the dollar was devalued. Steeply graduated income taxes were levied upon those who still had money and jobs. The NRA relaxed the anti-trust laws in the hope of benefiting business; and the Wagner Act conferred upon organized labor the "unique statutory power" that Arthur Krock has described.

So in the vernacular of the day, the government "shot the works"; and by 1938 the national debt was 2½ times the 1929 level, while federal expenditures had trebled. But still ten million people—19 per cent of the labor force—were unemployed. Then came Pearl Harbor; and unemployment vanished almost completely. But its scars did not.

With the return of peace, in 1945, the spectre of unemployment still haunted the memory of the nation; and when many leading economists and government officials incorrectly predicted another post-war depression, the shadow of that spectre lengthened darkly.

So it was under these circumstances, and against this background, that Congress passed the Employment Act of 1946 which committed the government to a policy of economic planning in support of maximum employment, and created the Council of Economic Advisers to give expert direction to the mobilization and use of the government's monetary and fiscal powers "in a manner calculated to foster and promote free competitive enterprise . . ."

Since then the government, under both political parties, has consciously pursued what has generally been an expansionary and moderately inflationary policy in accordance with the economic gospel of John Maynard Keynes. The money supply has been greatly enlarged, and until this year, the objective of the Council has been to stimulate demand at a rate that would require fuller utilization and expansion of the nation's productive capacity—thus providing more jobs. So while prices have both risen and fallen under the pressures of competition, of market demand, of fluctuations in the business cycle, and the "police action" in Korea, their trend has been upwards as the purchasing power of the dollar has steadily declined.

It should also be noted here, I think, that during this period the national economy has grown rapidly. Cyclical recessions have not disappeared; but they have been relatively mild and short-lived; and while the remaining "pockets of poverty" are a source of deep concern throughout the land, nothing remotely resembling the destitution of the 1930s has recurred. Never in the last quarter-century, in fact, has annual unemployment amounted to as much as 7 per cent of the labor force; and today, when that figure has dropped to 3.8 per cent, there is a real shortage of skilled workers.

At the same time, however, the cumulative effects of inflation—over these years—have confronted the government with new problems, both political and economic.

On the political side, the ever-rising cost of living is causing widespread consumer unrest; while on the economic side, the persistent imbalance of international payments and the steady drain on the nation's gold supply have become matters of deep concern to the government. Meanwhile, the national debt is more than 7½ times as large as it was in 1938, and federal expenditures alone have multiplied fourteenfold.

So today, after twenty years under the Employment Act of 1946, we come squarely up against the question of whether it is possible to have full employment without inflation. Many leading economists have pointed out that it has never been done in history; and in his recent testimony on Capitol Hill, Gardner Ackley, Chairman of the Council of Economic Advisers, declared: "The basic dilemma of reconciling high employment with price stability will persist, as it has in industrial nations throughout the world."

Certainly if maximum employment can be achieved only by increasing the nation's money supply more rapidly than its productive capacity, prices must ultimately, and inevitably, rise. Conversely, if it is necessary to maintain permanent reservoirs of idle manpower in order to prevent inflation, then those who advocate that course face a Herculean task in making their views politically acceptable.

Confronted by this dilemma, it was natural that government should temporize—as governments historically have—by trying to restrain rising prices without materially lessening the expansionary economic policies which were a fundamental cause of the problem.

And so in the 1962 report of the Council of Economic Advisers, the wage-price guideposts made their debut—more in the form of a trial balloon than as an established economic doctrine. But as their evolution has progressed through successive annual reports since then, their character has undergone a significant and disturbing change.

Evolution

In their original form, the guideposts were presented as a "suggested" means by which the public might judge whether a particular wage-price decision was in the national interest. They were intended, the authors said, "as a contribution to . . . widespread public discussion and clarification of the issues."

"These are not arbitrary guides," the Council cautioned. "Nor do they constitute a mechanical formula for determining whether a particular price or wage decision is inflationary. They will serve their purpose if they suggest to the interested public a useful way of approaching the appraisal of such a decision."

The Council also stated flatly that mandatory peacetime controls were neither desirable nor practical—that wages, benefits, and working conditions should be determined through collective bargaining and that "final price decisions lie—and should continue to lie—in the hands of individual firms."

The Economic Advisers were careful also to point out that while the rate of change in output per man hour, which they call productivity change, is an important benchmark, it should be a "*guide* rather than a *rule* for appraising wage and price behaviour." They added that "the pattern of wages and prices among industries is, and should be, responsive to forces other than changes in productivity."

So it was in the guise more of an educational exercise than of economic dictum that the now-familiar formulae for appraising wage and price behavior were presented.

Briefly, they laid down the general rule that the increase in wages and benefits in each industry should "equal" the trend rate of over-all, or national, productivity. And in individual industries where the increase in productivity was greater or less than the national trend rate, prices should fall or rise accordingly; otherwise, they should remain stable.

Again the Advisers warned, however, that "these are advanced as general guideposts" and that "specific modifications must be made to adapt them to the circumstances of particular industries." Public judgments, they said, "should take into account the modifications as well as the general guides."

Thereupon they proceeded to set forth numerous modifications, or exceptions, designed to cover some of the many factors, other than productivity, which might alter the applicability of the general guideposts to the specific circumstances in individual companies and industries. And this "fine print"—as it has been called— was so broad in scope as to make it appear that judgments affecting wages and prices in most industries would have to be made on a case-by-case basis.

It should be noted also that the council did not

attempt to present a figure fixing the national trend-rate of productivity increase; and its members were at great pains to explain the extreme difficulties inherent in making such a calculation.

But the guideposts have changed significantly in tone and in concept since that original version appeared nearly five years ago. No longer "suggested" guides, they had become "standards" in the language of the 1965 report. The exceptions that were to have been part and parcel of the basic formulae had faded; and the 1964 report declares that the general guideposts "can cover the vast majority of wage and price decisions," and that the modifications are "intended to apply to only a relatively few cases." In the current 1966 report some of these modifications, in fact, are no longer mentioned at all.

Similarly their "voluntary" nature has given way to an increasing measure of compulsion. The 1964 report warns that "The administration will not hesitate to call public attention" to wage or price decisions that "seriously overstep" non-inflationary "standards." And the current report carries the thought of sanctions much further by declaring that "defense procurement, agricultural and other policies will be adjusted where necessary to avoid contributing to instability of prices."

Meanwhile, in the 1964 edition, the council managed to resolve all its methodological doubts about the national trend of productivity increase, and reported that it was precisely 3.2 per cent. In the following year, the same method of calculation yielded exactly the same figure; but for this year it would have produced a higher figure of 3.6 per cent, and the council concluded that this would not be an accurate measure of the true long-term trend of productivity. It also pointed out that the increased Social Security and Medicare taxes had added about two-thirds of 1 per cent to employment costs, and that this legislated increase in benefits was not included in the definition of employee compensation for guidepost purposes. It therefore decreed that the magic number of 3.2 per cent should stand unchanged.

So gradually, over these years, the guideposts have been transformed from an educational tool into something resembling a Procrustean bed to the dimensions of which wages and prices are henceforth expected to conform; and it is in this present guise that their virtues and their faults must be appraised.

Appraisal

From a business point of view, their greatest virtue lies in focusing public attention upon the immutable fact that whenever employment costs rise more rapidly than productivity, as they have consistently in most of the post-war years, then—other things being equal—production costs will increase accordingly and will be reflected in rising prices to the extent that competitive forces of the market place permit.

They have also demonstrated fairly conclusively, I think, how impotent government is, under existing laws, to cope with those "unique powers of organized labor to raise the costs of production virtually at will." While the Administration has successfully used its "moral suasion" to prevent or curtail price increases in some highly-visible industries such as steel, aluminum, and copper, I am aware of few similar instances of success in respect to rising wages. In fact, settlements in major manufacturing industries last year recorded an average increase of 4 per cent in wages alone—substantially above the 3.2 per cent limit set forth in the guideposts for wages and benefits together. And this year they have ranged materially above that. So as an educational tool, the guideposts have, at least, provided an important lesson in the "cost-push" type of inflation and its causes, if not its cure.

On the other side of the coin, so many outstanding economists have found so many faults in the guideposts that within the scope of this paper it is possible to cover only the most important of these. So let us look first at the wage side, then at the price side, and finally at the difficulties inherent in the over-all guidepost philosophy.

Wage Guideposts

One major weakness in the guidepost approach to wages is the underlying supposition that public opinion, duly alerted, can and will act to restrain excesses. There is no doubt that public opinion is a powerful force in our society; but pitted against union power, it has been singularly ineffective. In the case of the New York subway strike early this year, and again in the case of the airlines strike a few months ago, public opinion was vocally outraged, but its influence was scarcely detectable because there was no way for it to be mobilized at a specific pressure point. So the settlements, when they were reached, greatly exceeded the guidepost limitations, even though in the airlines controversy, top administration officials participated in the negotiations.

A second basic flaw lies in the use of the national productivity trend as the standard intended to govern wage increases in each individual industry. This obscures the link between economic performance and economic reward. As Dr. Gordon McKinley, Vice President-Economics of McGraw-Hill, has put it:

> It does not matter whether workers in a particular firm or industry work hard or not, or intelligently or not, or effectively or not; it does not matter whether the consumer desires their product or not; it does not matter whether management . . . is effective or not; it does not matter whether technology advances rapidly or not. The economic reward for all members in this industry is specifically held to the economic performance of the economy as a whole.

Now labor leaders who hold elective office in their unions have political problems too. Naturally they would like to be re-elected at the expiration of their terms; but how will the guideposts affect their political chances?

In a company where the productivity increase was 2 per cent, for example, the employees would still get a 3.2 per cent increase because that is the guidepost figure. And doubtless the membership would be very happy with this windfall; but the government, rather than the labor leader, would get most of the credit for it.

In a company where productivity had risen 5 per cent, however, the union leaders would supposedly settle for a 3.2 per cent wage increase because that is the "ceiling" provided in the guideposts. The union leaders might understand the economics of it, but how are they going to sell it to their membership? And even more importantly—if wage settlements are going to be determined automatically by a guidepost formula, who needs a union anyway? What will be its role in the future?

So the idea of linking wages in individual industries or companies to the national productivity trend is somewhat impractical to say the least. But unfortunately, it is no more so than the alernative policy of linking wages in each company, industry or service to the individual productivity trends in those groups.

For example, waiters, barbers, TV repairmen, and people in similar occupations where there can be little or no increase in productivity, would never improve their wages and would thus soon turn to other fields of employment. And what wage scale should prevail in a craft union whose members work in many different industries with differing rates of productivity? Clearly, this course, too, presents insurmountable obstacles.

A third difficulty with the wage guideposts is their failure to distinguish between productivity and output per man hour. The two are by no means the same.

To illustrate with a simple hypothetical example: It is possible to enrich the iron ore going into a blast furnace and thus to step up the production of the furnace without increasing the number of men in the crew. Let us suppose that this increase in output per man hour reduces the labor cost of the smelted iron by a dollar a ton. But the cost of enriching the ore was—let us say— fifty cents per ton of iron produced. Thus the gain in productivity—out of which higher wages could come —was only fifty cents, not a dollar.

So wherever increased production results from better facilities, improved technology, or any cause other than the greater effort and skill of the worker himself, productivity improvement will always be less than the increase in output per man hour as reported in the guideposts.

And finally, two further difficulties with the wage guideposts should be noted. The first is that they would freeze the percentage of the national income which goes to labor at its present level, which may or may not be the most economically advantageous level for the nation. And second, they would tend to discourage the normal and desirable flow of workers from declining to expanding industries. Normally, wages in declining businesses would lag behind the parade, while those in expanding companies would rise more rapidly and thus attract the lower-paid workers into the new jobs that are opening up. But by the deadly process of leveling out all wage increases, the incentive to change jobs in accordance with the productive needs of the nation is greatly diminished.

In summary, it appears that the wage guideposts tend to discourage or destroy individual incentive, to threaten the political security of union leaders, and to interfere with the normal flow of workers from job to job.

Price Guideposts

On the price side, the first question that arises is whether it is possible to comply with the guideposts at all, however much a producer may wish to do so. Under the prescribed formula, he is supposed to compare the productivity trend in his own individual operation with the national 3.2 average, and adjust his prices accordingly. But productivity differs widely among industries; it differs among companies within an industry and among plants within a company; and beyond that it differs among operations and products within a plant. On what basis, then, is the productivity trend to be calculated in his case? There are no adequate government statistics to guide him; and there is little possibility that they could be developed over a sufficiently broad range.

Suppose, however, that from his own records he is able conscientiously to calculate a productivity figure and that this is below 3.2 per cent. The guideposts decree that he is entitled to raise his prices; but what will the market place say about it? What if competitive conditions make a price rise impossible? He is still saddled with a wage increase that the guideposts have virtually compelled him to grant.

If, on the other hand, he finds that productivity in his operation is above 3.2 per cent, he is supposed to reduce his prices. But at what hazard? Will he be able to increase them again in a later year if productivity has then changed, or will market conditions or a new set of government rules prevent him from doing so? And what about improvements in the quality of his product? Must they be ignored under the price formula?

These simple questions, I believe, point up a glaring and irreparable fault in the price guideposts. By linking prices solely to wages and productivity, they ignore and defy the immutable law of supply and demand; and in place of market competition, they would substitute what Dr. McKinley terms "a cost-plus economy."

We know that whenever demand for a particular product or service exceeds supply, the price will be bid up —as it should be; for by rising, it performs an economic service to society that can be achieved in no other way. The higher price induces the supplier to increase his output, while the rising profit margin attracts others into the business; and supply thus grows to meet the demand.

Meanwhile, the rising price has performed an important rationing function by encouraging those who can turn to a substitute product or service to do so, thus leaving the limited available supply for those who are most in need of it.

Conversely, of course, an excess of supply over demand intensifies competition, depresses prices and profits, and discourages the wasteful use of the nation's resources of manpower, materials, and capital in the production of unwanted products or services.

In this way prices act as a kind of non-electronic computer which, under the sole direction of the customer, channels the nation's resources most efficiently into the production of the things most wanted. The market place itself decides whether a price increase is "justified" or not; and it is the only tribunal that is equipped to do so—

as even Soviet Russia has come to recognize recently. Yet the guideposts would seize this power from 115 million adult American consumers and give it to government where the infinitely complex economic factors involved in reaching a judgment would be further complicated by political considerations as well.

Will it be politically possible for government officials, for example, to give recognition to the fact that too low a price can be just as contrary to the public interest as one that is too high?

And if government monopoly is to be substituted for market place competition, must not some federal agency then be created to raise investment capital and to regulate and direct its flow throughout the economy?

What happens, too, to the anti-trust concept? Is it proper and lawful for any group of competitors in bargaining jointly with a national union representing their employees, to conclude a wage agreement from which it is implicitly understood that the prices of all of them will rise, or fall, or remain unchanged as the guideposts may require?

And finally, there is the basic question as to why there should be any price formula in the guideposts at all. If there is any justification for guideposts, it would seemingly lie in fact that wages have consistently climbed year after year—in times of rising productivity and of falling productivity, in times of high employment and of high unemployment, in prosperity and in recessions, and in peace and in war. And the indications of the existence of union monopoly power are thus clear.

But prices are subject to their own rigid discipline

in the market place, and the fact that countless numbers of them rise and fall daily in response to competitive pressures would seem to demonstrate with equal clarity that monopoly does not exist in the free and voluntary exchange of goods and services between buyer and seller.

So it would appear that the price formula was included in the guideposts as a matter of political propriety rather than of economic desirability.

Underlying Faults

Underlying the many faults we have noted in the application of the wage-price formulae, however, are a number of serious flaws in the basic concept of the guideposts as a whole. As a matter of fairness, for example, they should deal equitably with all segments of the economy; and if they have any restraining effect upon prices at all, this should clearly be exercised in the area of food and services where prices last year and this have increased most steeply, rather than in the industrial sector where the prices of durable goods have not increased at all. The government's Consumer Price Index shows that between January of last year and August of this year, food prices have risen 8.6 per cent, and services 5.5 per cent, while the price of durable goods has declined six-tenths of one per cent.

But the guideposts do not cover all segments of the economy, nor is it intended that they should. There seems to be no practical way to apply them to the producers of food and the purveyors of services, nor can their creators hope to keep vigil over all of the hundreds of thousands of producing units in the industrial area.

Since the guideposts have not been successfully applied
to unions either large or small, it follows that their effect
is confined to only a limited number of companies in a
few highly-visible industries. No one knows which ones
or how many.

A second, more serious, flaw has become evident,
moreover, as the character of the guideposts has changed
over the years. No longer "suggested" behavioral guides,
they have become an instrument for the attempted control of prices without any of the safeguards encompassed
in the phrase "due process of law." They were not
created by legislative authority, nor after public hearings
where persons affected could express their views. No
penalties are prescribed for those who are deemed to
have violated the rules; and there is no place to which
persons accused of such violations can appeal. Enforcement depends, therefore, on what one leading economist
has called "undue process." W. Allen Wallis, who is
now President of the University of Rochester, puts it
this way:

> Violators . . . are not prosecuted for the viola-
> tions. Instead, every law, regulation or requirement
> to which the offender is subject, however unrelated
> to the offense, may be searched for some possible
> violation—a process which, even if it leads to
> nothing, constitutes in itself a heavy penalty in time,
> money, fear, and notoriety. Every benefit or privilege
> which the offender may derive, directly or indirectly,
> from the Government may be withdrawn—or the
> fear of withdrawal used to secure compliance.

Now this lack of due process clearly stands as a
serious threat to freedom; but I am also concerned about

the fact that it leads to attempted enforcement by a process of confrontation in which both the government and the company involved must ultimately lose face. When companies or industries are publicly denounced and excoriated, or are otherwise forced to comply with the CEA's wishes, the reverberations are felt throughout the business community, and a wedge is thus driven between business and government at a time in our history when better understanding and closer cooperation between the two is of paramount necessity.

Equally of concern to me is the fact that when presidential authority is successfully defied, as it has been so consistently on the wage side, the resulting blow to the prestige of the President and to the dignity of his high office can hardly fail to have an effect upon the moral fiber of the nation and to undermine respect for government generally. Precisely because widespread and continuing defiance of presidential authority is politically intolerable, the guideposts are leading us more and more in the direction of legislated price and wage controls, followed—as inevitably they must be—by rationing, black markets, and the suppression of the freedoms—economic and political—which have made our nation the most productive on earth.

This, I believe, is the end of the road to which the guideposts now point; and it is a road that we must not follow. It is the road that has led so many nations to disaster when their governments have sought—as the guideposts do—to attack the symptoms of inflation instead of the causes of the disease. President Wallis makes this point emphatically when he says:

Inflation can be generated only by government. Business firms, labor unions, or consumers with excessive market power can do many objectionable things that are contrary to the public interest; but one objectionable thing that they cannot do is to cause inflation—or, for that matter, prevent it. . . . There is one, and only one, way to achieve the price stability at which the guidelines purport to aim, and that is to control the rate of growth in the stock of money and credit.

Some others who hold this view have contended that if we did not already have guideposts in existence when inflation began to cause public concern, it would have been politically necessary for government to invent them as a means of shifting the blame to other segments of the society.

In fact, one of the dangers which several leading economists cite in connection with the guideposts is that by using them to focus blame on business and labor, the government may successfully evade its own politically-unpalatable responsibility to correct the root causes of inflation. And in a scholarly analysis of the guideposts which was published in the *Harvard Business Review* last year, Dr. Arthur Burns—himself a former chairman of the Council of Economic Advisers—declared that a "major need of our times is for better guidelines to aid the government itself in formulating and carrying out its economic policies."

Noting that general observance of the guideposts "would throttle the forces of competition no less effectively than those of monopoly"; and that "free competitive markets would virtually cease to exist," he wrote:

"A government that is seriously concerned about inflation will not pursue an expansive monetary and fiscal policy at such a time, and—instead of lecturing the private community on the need for moderation—will itself lead the nation in a policy of restraint."

The Guideposts Today

For all of these reasons, the guidepost mechanism today is in a state of suspended animation. Labor stands in open revolt against the 3.2 per cent wage ceiling, and its leaders have voiced their defiance of the guideposts both in words and in deeds. Confronted by this fact of life, the administration seems no longer to be making any serious effort to hold wage increases at that level. A. H. Raskin, that knowledgeable labor expert of *The New York Times*, writes:

Informally, the new holding position [of the Government] has been established at 5 per cent—the level that emerged from mediation under White House auspices in last summer's strike of machinists against five large airlines. Fumbling, rather than design, accounted for that figure, but it has now become the threshhold of expectation for all other strong unions and the Administration cannot disown it.

And he predicts that next year will be an even stormier one on the labor front, with rising strike turbulence.

So once again, the government has reached what might accurately be called a moment of indecision. To attempt to cling to the unworkable guidepost mechanisms would be futile, fruitless and frustrating at best; and certainly it would be disastrous, in my opinion, to turn further toward outright controls by attempting to freeze wages and prices, as has been done in England, to enforce the "Incomes Policy" which is the British version of the guideposts.

But with employment costs soaring far above productivity gains and with new pressures thus building up under prices, what are the economically constructive courses which can be pursued?

Suggested Remedies

To most economists, I believe, the obvious course would be to reverse the expansionary monetary and fiscal policies that have prevailed throughout the postwar years —to constrict the supply of money and credit, to syphon off excess purchasing power in the hands of the consumer, and to curtail government spending in non-defense areas. By stretching out numerous welfare programs in this period of economic boom, a backlog upon which to draw in times of economic slack would be created.

This course, however, arouses no political enthusiasm whatever among most of those who hold elective office at any level of government. In his congressional testimony, Chairman Ackley said: "We will surely not be willing to sacrifice this goal [of full employment and steady growth] and to maintain a reserve army of unemployed and idle machines in order to enforce discipline on areas where markets operate imperfectly."

But in a speech last month before the National Industrial Conference Board where he outlined his fiscal objectives for next year, he made it plain that the government should relax the pressure it has been putting on the economic accelerator.

> Our objective must be to maintain the growth of the real GNP in line with the growth of our physical capacity to produce. . . . Over the past 5½ years, real GNP has expanded at an average rate close to 5½ per cent a year. Through this process we have brought our economy as close to full utilization of its resources as can safely be accomplished by measures operating on the side of aggregate demand. Now demand expansion must only be adequate to support a 4 per cent real GNP growth. . . .

And on October 26th, Chairman Ackley had reached the point of view that additional attempts to reduce unemployment by stimulating over-all demand would involve "a substantial cost in terms of inflationary pressures." At this point in time, he believes that the best way to reduce unemployment involves "measures to make the remaining unemployed more suitable to the kinds of jobs that today's economy—and tomorrow's—will demand."

Regardless of how you construe this statement by the Chairman of the CEA, it encourages the hope that so far as the vast economic power of government is concerned, its pressure on expansionary policies and hence on prices will gradually be reduced; but this still leaves the cost-push effects of excessive increases in wages and benefits.

Most businessmen who have faced the "unique statutory power of organized labor" at the bargaining table will agree, I believe, that it overwhelmingly outweighs any powers which the industry bargainers can command in the negotiating process. Apparently it also exceeds—as events have shown—all the power that government can muster in its efforts to hold settlement terms in line with productivity trends.

To revise the statutes so as to restore some semblance of balance between the powers of union and of management negotiators at the bargaining table, would be the obvious solution of this fundamental problem—if it were politically possible. And in view of the mounting resentment of a strike-unhappy public against the willful and ill considered use of the strike weapon against the public itself, I am by no means sure that a sincere and courageous effort in this direction would not arouse widespread support within the electorate and yield political rewards rather than penalties. But as I said earlier, I am not a politician.

Assuming, therefore, that there is no practical prospect of achieving this kind of a solution—at least until and unless the dangers of inflation become far more compelling than they are today—it seems to me that there still is one course of action which the administration and the members of Congress could pursue without undue political risk, and which they must pursue, I believe, if the seemingly irreconcilable differences between good politics and good economics are ever to be erased. And that is to lay before the public—*in meaningful terms*—the simple economic facts about wages and profits.

At a time when the government is urging responsible leaders of labor to exercise restraint in enforcing their wage demands, it is difficult for me to understand why, during the past few months, administration leaders—including the President and members of his cabinet—have publicized the fact so widely that since 1960 total corporate profits have risen much more rapidly, in terms of percentage, than have wages.

Encouraged by the publicity accorded to these official statements, George Meany, President of the AFL-CIO, has given them further currency in support of his contention that this is a "profit inflation—pure and simple." And doubtless most union members and many members of the public have thus been led to believe that labor has been getting the short end of the stick and is entitled to the large pay increases it has been demanding.

Now the facts upon which these statements have been based are that during the five years from 1960 to 1965, aggregate corporate profits have risen 67 per cent, while total employee compensation has increased only 34 per cent—or merely half as fast.

But suppose that instead of simply using percentages —which are notoriously misleading when one is applied to a very large base and another to a very small base— the administration had emphasized the fact that total corporate profits, during this period, had risen by 18 billion dollars, while total compensation of employees had risen by 99 billion dollars—or 5½ times as much as profits. Would not this comparison have been more meaningful—especially since inflation flows from money —not from percentages? These are the official government figures from which the percentages were calculated, and certainly they would have given the public a picture very different from the one that has been presented in these administration statements.

Moreover, one may wonder why the administration officials, in these statements, chose to use 1960, a year of recession, as the basis for their comparisons with the present period of record prosperity. This is the kind of comparison which conscientious statisticians seek to avoid, recognizing that fair and valid analyses must take into account the fluctuations in the business cycle, so that good years are likened to good years, and poor ones, to poor ones.

So if we compare the good year of 1950 with the good year 1955, we find that total corporate profits rose by 2 billion dollars, while total employee compensation increased 70 billion dollars—or 35 times as much.

Taking the next five year period and comparing the good year of 1955 with the recession year of 1960, we find that corporate profits declined by 300 million dollars while employee compensation still increased by 70 billion dollars.

And if we look at the entire fifteen-year period, comparing prosperous 1950 with prosperous 1965, we see that corporate profits grew by about 19½ billion dollars while employee compensation rose 238 billions—or more than 12 times as much. Even the use of percentages cannot obscure the commanding advantage which labor has enjoyed over this fifteen-year period, for corporate profits rose 79 per cent while employee compensation increased 154 per cent.

A much more meaningful use of percentages, however, is to compare the respective shares of the total national income that go to employee compensation and to profits—for here the percentages in each year apply to exactly the same base on both sides. And looking at the facts in this way, we see that in 1950, 10.3 per cent of the national income went to profits, while in 1965 that figure had dropped to 8 per cent. Conversely, the share of the national income that went to employee compensation in 1950 was 64.1 per cent and by 1965 had risen to 70.3 per cent.

So the employee share has expanded by 6.2 percentage points, while the profit share has been squeezed down by 2.3 percentage points—a fact that should surely spread great joy throughout the halls of labor, but that certainly dispels the erroneous notion that profits have flourished at the expense of wages.

One may also wonder why administration spokesmen have not seen fit to emphasize the fact that wage increases have vastly outstripped rises in the cost of living over the years—especially since the union drive to force escalation clauses into newly negotiated contracts is a major bone of contention at the bargaining table today.

These escalation clauses—which provide for automatic wage increases geared to the rise in the cost of living—are, economically speaking, engines of inflation which impart perpetual motion to the whirling wage-price spiral; but union bargainers point to the currently-rapid rise in the Consumer Price Index as justification for their refusal to exercise the restraint that government has asked of them.

Yet the fact is that since 1950, the cost of living has gone up 37 per cent while hourly earnings have climbed 82 per cent, which means that in terms of actual purchasing power, the earnings of the worker have risen by 33 per cent. Someone in high office may have pointed out that salient fact, but if so, it has escaped my attention, and certainly it has not been generally publicized.

So the point I should like to make in conclusion is this: When a businessman presents these facts, as I have here today, his voice is heard only by an infinitesimal few; and cynics among these few may discard them as being "self-serving." But the president, the members of his cabinet, and the members of Congress can reach the ears and the eyes of vast numbers of people, and because of the respected offices they hold their statements are widely discussed and believed.

To a degree that no one else enjoys, therefore, they have the power to bring economic understanding of the facts about inflation to all of the thoughtful citizens in the land; and if they fully discharge what I regard as a compelling obligation to exercise this power, the day may hopefully come when the voting public will be so well informed that it will no longer be possible for bad economics to be good politics. For only when good economics becomes good politics can the age-old problem of inflation be laid to rest without the loss of human freedom.

This I believe.

WAGE-PRICE GUIDEPOSTS AS AN INSTRUMENT TO ATTAIN U.S. ECONOMIC GOALS *

by Neil H. Jacoby

DEAN

GRADUATE SCHOOL OF BUSINESS ADMINISTRATION,
UNIVERSITY OF CALIFORNIA AT LOS ANGELES

* I thank my colleagues F. Meyers, S. H. Nerlove, F. E. Norton, and J. F. Weston for helpful comments upon an earlier draft of this essay.

THE GUIDEPOSTS for non-inflationary wage and price behavior proposed by President Kennedy in January 1962
have had a stormy career.[1] They were elevated to the
status of a major instrument of U.S. economic policy by
President Johnson in January 1966.[2] During recent years
both presidents have said repeatedly that adherence to
the guideposts by labor and business executives was a
test of their "responsibility" and "concern for the public
interest." Reputable economists have defended them as a
supplementary instrument of control. Yet the guideposts
were often breached, and governmental efforts to enforce them finally foundered on the shoals of inflationary

---

1 *Economic Report of the President to the Congress of January
  1962* (Washington, U.S. Government Printing Office, 1962),
  pp. 185–90.
2 *Economic Report of the President to the Congress of January
  1966* (Washington, U.S. Government Printing Office, 1966),
  pp. 88–93.

demand during 1966, as some predicted.[3] Today, most Americans probably believe that the guideposts are a desirable instrument of economic policy which, though ineffective in preventing inflation, have at least done the economy no harm. President Johnson has announced that an effort will be made to find another kind of guidepost for controlling wages and prices.

Prevailing views about the role and effects of the guideposts are confused and disturbing in their implications. In the welter of published comment about this new instrument of economic policy, there has been little fundamental analysis. The time has come to ask some basic questions. Should the guideposts be viewed like Prohibition—as a "noble experiment" that failed because of business and labor recalcitrance? What influence have they really had upon the attainment of our national goals? Are direct governmental controls of wages and prices —with or without benefit of statutory authority—desirable in the present U.S. economy? Are there better ways to resolve the problem of attaining full employment and rapid growth without price inflation in a market-directed economy?

I wish to examine these issues from the point of

3 This writer's forecast that the guideposts would fail to prevent substantial price inflation during 1966 was published in *The UCLA Business Forecast for the Nation and Southern California in 1966* (Los Angeles, Graduate School of Business Administration, UCLA, December 8, 1965), and in a statement on "Wage-Price Guideposts versus Monetary and Fiscal Policies to Attain Full Employment Without Inflation" to the Joint Economic Committee of the Congress. See *Hearings on the January 1966 Economic Report of the President* before the Joint Economic Committee, February 10, 1966. (Washington, U.S. Government Printing Office, 1966), pp. 472–78.

view of the public interest. A university economist should, at least, be able to consider them without bias. He has no stockholders to face, no union members to placate, no voters to please. First, let us review the basic theory of the guideposts and trace their evolution into a major tool of the "New Economics." Next, let us define the goals of "full employment" and "price-level stability" in operationally useful terms. Then, we shall assess the true magnitude of the problem of reconciling our employment and price-level targets. Finally, we shall propose governmental policies for raising the employment ratio, without at the same time lowering productivity, provoking general price inflation, or impairing the traditional freedoms of our people.

Theoretical Foundations of the Guideposts

Guideposts to non-inflationary wage and price behavior were proposed in President Kennedy's *Economic Report of January 1962* in a well-meaning effort to help solve an important economic problem. This was the persistent tendency of the price level to rise, even when there were substantial numbers of unemployed people seeking work and many industrial plants operating well under their designed capacities. To be sure, price inflation during the late fifties and early sixties was negligible, averaging under one and one-half per cent a year in the Consumer Price Index during the five-year period 1957–61. Yet the Consumer Price Index had risen more rapidly during the three relatively prosperous years 1955–1957, when unemployment averaged a low 4.3 per cent of the labor force. Moreover, it was correctly foreseen that, as the economy responded to the expansionary fiscal and monetary measures of the new administration, of which the massive tax reduction made in January 1964 was the most spectacular, stronger upward pressures upon prices would be generated as slack was taken up. Americans now properly assign a high priority to a dollar of stable buying power. They reject even "creeping inflation" as an acceptable condition.[4]

The classical explanation of general price inflation is that of "demand-pull"—a condition of total monetary demand for goods and services exceeding the capacity of the economy to produce them, and leading to a general marking-up of prices. The classical method of stopping inflation is to impose fiscal and monetary restraints upon the growth of aggregate demand, to the point where it does not exceed the rate of aggregate supply, at current prices. Clearly, the classical theory failed to explain a general rise in prices that occurred even when, by general agreement, unused productive capacity remained in the economy.

The initial theoretical foundation for the guideposts was the concept of "cost-push" inflation. This was a general rise in prices generated by the ability of powerful

4 A subtle change in attitudes has taken place during the last decade. Few economists defend creeping inflation today, whereas many did during the Fifties. See, for example, Sumner Slichter, "On the Side of Inflation," *Harvard Business Review* (September–October, 1957) in response to this author's "The Threat of Inflation," *Harvard Business Review* (May–June, 1957), and this author's "Letter to the Editor," *Harvard Business Review* (January–February, 1958).

labor unions to raise wages, or of monopolistic business firms to raise prices, under conditions of less than full employment. Price inflation was seen as a consequence of inordinate power over labor and commodity markets by private economic groups. While admitting the existence of such market power, particularly in the hands of well-organized labor unions, critics of the "cost-push" theory were quick to point out that cost-push alone could not produce a *sustained* general price inflation. Unless our monetary and fiscal managers expanded aggregate demand for goods and services to levels that permitted the public to pay the higher prices produced by rising wage-costs per unit, the cost-push on prices would be brought to a halt. Both "demand-pull" and "cost-push" are necessary to enable price inflation to continue for long. But the "cost" of price-level stability, so attained, would be an unacceptably high unemployment ratio.

The implication of accepting "cost-push" as a material cause of inflation was that a new instrument of policy would be needed to prevent price inflation from starting before conditions of full employment were reached. This new instrument might seek to reduce private market power and the downward inflexibility of wages and prices, or it might accept such conditions and seek to prevent their inflationary consequences. The latter course appeared to be politically easier and more prompt in its effects. Federal enforcement of "guideposts" to wage and price changes was the chosen instrument.

An even broader theoretical foundation for the guideposts was laid in the *Study of Employment, Growth and*

Price Levels conducted for the Joint Economic Committee in 1959.[5] This study inquired into the causes of the
1955–57 price inflation which took place during a boom
in the capital goods industries, but with no excessive demand in the aggregate. Clearly, the inflation of 1955–57
was not the simple classical case of "demand-pull" inflation, because employment was not full. Nor did it appear
to correspond to the pure case of "cost-push" inflation,
because the particular economic sectors in which wages
and prices rose most conspicuously—the metals and
machinery industries—were fully employed. The study
brought forth the idea of "demand-shift" inflation. According to this concept, a general rise in prices may be
generated simply by the dynamics of shifting demand
and resource allocation. Given the downward rigidity of
many wage-rates and prices in the U.S. economy, a strong
rise of demand in one sector may produce increases in
the wage-rates and prices of that sector, that are not
offset by reductions in other sectors where demand has
not risen or has even fallen. A rise in average prices
(that is, in the price index) then ensues, even in the face
of unemployment in many parts of the economy.

The policy implications of the "demand-shift" theory
are, at first blush, startling. It would appear that, even if
the inordinate market power of labor unions and big
corporations could be brought within acceptable limits,
dynamic changes in our economy make inflation in-

5 See *Staff Report on Employment, Growth and Price Levels.*
Joint Economic Committee of the Congress, particularly Study
Paper No. 1 "Recent Inflation in the United States" by Charles
L. Schultze. (Washington, U.S. Government Printing Office,
1959).

evitable. The twin goals of full employment and a stable price level are unattainable. However, closer analysis does not lead to this melancholy conclusion. The resistance of wage-rates and prices to reductions in industries having inadequate demand, which is a fundamental premise of the "demand-shift" theory, is mainly dependent upon the private market power of some large labor unions and corporations, supplemented by governmental price-supporting programs. If these causes were eliminated, some wage-rates and prices would decline, and the average of all prices would not necessarily rise.

More important is the fact that productivity in the private economy has been rising more than three per cent a year. Average annual wage-rate increases up to this amount are offset by an average rise in output per man hour, producing *no* change in costs per unit, or in prices based on such costs. So long as productivity rises briskly, the American economy can tolerate a considerable amount of market power, downward rigidity of wages, and even general wage increases resulting from shifts in demand, without suffering price inflation. If private market power and cost-push are too great to be offset by productivity gains, the basic solution, obviously, is to reduce it to tolerable levels rather than to suppress its consequences.

In an expanding economy, some industries and sectors nearly always expand more rapidly than others. So long as wage-rates, prices, and resource movements are not perfectly flexible, these industries form "bottlenecks" to continued general growth. We can now see that "demand-shift" and "cost-push" are really two labels for an

inflationary process put into motion by the same structural causes.[6] They are not really separate theories of
inflation. Not surprisingly, they have both led to the conclusion that government must intervene directly to prevent wage increases in excess of average productivity
gains. They rationalize the present administration's
strategy of highly stimulative fiscal measures, combined
with direct controls of "key" wages and prices, in order
to attain full employment without inflation. Indeed, the
guideposts were intended to allay public opposition to
expansionist fiscal and monetary policies.

Evolution of the Guideposts

Private market power, rigid prices, and "cost-
push" inflation are not, of course, new phenomena in the
U.S. economy. Neither are the efforts of American presidents to repress it. Hortatory or "jawbone" controls of
upward wage and price thrusts were periodically employed by Presidents Eisenhower and Truman. What was
new about the guideposts was, first, the specification of
a *formula* by which to judge non-inflationary wage and
price increases, and secondly, efforts by federal officials
to *enforce* the formula. The original presentation of the
guideposts in the *Economic Report* of January 1962 was
tentative and judicious. After asserting that "there are
important segments of the economy where firms are large

6 This point is well made by Professor Gottfried Haberler in
Inflation—Its Causes and Cures, Revised and Enlarged Edition
(Washington, American Enterprise Institute for Public Policy
Research, 1966), p. 12.

or employees well-organized and there is considerable room for the exercise of private power" in wage and price decisions that affect the public interest, the report rejected mandatory direct controls in peacetime. It proposed that productivity be used as a "benchmark" for enabling the public to judge whether particular wage and price decisions were in the national interest. The *general guide* to wage behavior was that the annual percentage increase in the wages of each industry should equal the trend rate of increase in output per man hour of the economy. The *general guide* to price behavior was that prices in an industry should decline to the extent that productivity in the industry rose more than in the economy as a whole, and should rise to the degree that productivity in the industry rose less than in the economy. Adherence to these two rules would result in a stable price level over time, and in an average wage level that rose *pari passu* with the average national gain in productivity.

Less well known to the public—and in practice neglected in their application—were the important *modifications* of the general guides specified in the 1962 *Economic Report* as "necessary to attain equity and efficiency in the economy." The rise in the wages of an industry could be greater than that called for by the general guide, if its labor supply were deficient, or if its wages were relatively low; and it should be smaller if the industry's labor supply were redundant or its wages were relatively high. Price reductions in an industry should be less than permitted by the general guide, if its profit rate were insufficient to attract capital required for a needed expansion of capacity, or if its non-labor costs had risen: they should be greater if the industry possessed redundant capacity, its non-labor costs had fallen, or if its rate of return on investment were excessive.

The 1962 *Economic Report* recognized the great complexities of applying the guides to specific cases. It was careful to label them as "guides" rather than "rules." It stressed use of the guideposts *by the public* in judging the propriety of wage and price behavior. It did not intimate that federal officials would seek to apply them. Few would object to the use of guideposts simply as a basis of discussion and public education in wage-price-productivity relationships. Used only as educational devices, they could compel a deeper examination by labor and management officials of their own long-run interests.

It was not long, however, before high economic officials of the administration attempted to use the general guideposts as enforceable rules, with little attention paid to the vitally important modifications. These efforts were not conspicuous before 1965, when general economic expansion brought the unemployment ratio down close to the 4 per cent "interim" target set in President Kennedy's 1962 *Economic Report*. The Consumer Price Index rose very little during 1962–65, although the wholesale price index began to mount in 1965. The steel wage and price settlement of 1965, in which the administration intervened forcibly, was consistent with the guideposts; presidential pressure on the aluminum companies in October of 1965 caused them to rescind announced price increases.

In the January 1966 *Economic Report*, the administration glowingly described the guideposts as "a major innovation." It claimed that they had "gained increasing significance." It affirmed a "strong commitment to the guideposts as an essential pillar for price stability." Historical studies show that wage increases were indeed smaller during 1962–65 than during previous periods of economic expansion. But this does not prove that the guideposts were effective in restraining inflation. The more valid explanation of relative price stability during 1962–65 was the margin of slack in the economy, strong foreign competition in the steel and other industries, and, above all, stable price expectations of the public.

The January 1966 *Economic Report* established a general guidepost for wage increases during 1966 of 3.2 per cent.[7] It denied any need to modify this general wage guidepost by asserting that "the industries in which unions possess strong market power are largely high-wage industries in which job opportunities are relatively very attractive." It denied any need to modify the general price guidepost by the cavalier assertion that "the large firms to which the guideposts are primarily addressed typically have ready access to sources of capital; moreover, the profits of virtually every industry have risen sharply and are at record levels." Such slipshod reasoning no doubt contributed to the breakdown of the guideposts soon thereafter.

---

7 This number was arrived at by changing the previously-used time period over which the trend rate of productivity increase in the economy was measured, a change that was bitterly attacked by labor leaders.

Administrative Flaws in the Guideposts

We shall make only brief reference to the manifold theoretical flaws of the guideposts and to the fatal difficulties that arise in administering them. These problems are inherent in any scheme of governmental control of wages and prices in a competitive market economy, as we should have learned from our experience with direct controls during World War II and the Korean War. Several theoretical faults stand out. There is first the fundamental question why *all* of the gains from rising output per man hour should go to workers via increased wages, and none to consumers via a decline in prices. The measure of the trend rate of future productivity gains is *too indefinite* to provide a valid rule. One may debate endlessly—and inconclusively—such issues as the past time-period likely to be most representative of the future, and over what sectors of the economy productivity changes should be measured. Moreover, guideposts should apply to individual firms and not to "industries" in an age in which the rise of conglomerate firms has blurred the meaning of an "industry" in many parts of the economy.[8]

Thorny conceptual problems are compounded by the practical difficulties of government wage and price fixing. How can federal officials truly *measure* the relative

8 Technical faults of the guideposts are cogently discussed in the *News Letter* of the Management Development and Employee Relations Service of the General Electric Company (New York, August 13, 1963).

adequacy of the labor supply of a firm, whether its wages are relatively "high" or "low," how its non-labor costs have moved, whether its productive physical assets are excessive or deficient, or the proper level of its rate of return on investment? To deny the need to modify general wage or price rules on the ground that modifications are irrelevant in the U.S. economy of 1966—as was done in the January 1966 *Economic Report*—is to risk serious injustice and misallocation of resources.

On the other hand, to attempt to apply these modifications to individual firms in our huge and complex economy is to saddle the federal government with the impossible problems of detailed enterprise control from which the government of the centrally-planned Soviet economy is now trying to extricate itself![9] It is simply not feasible for governmental officials to fix equitable and efficient wage and price ceilings for individual enterprises in a large, dynamic market economy. Markets are too numerous, too complex, and change too rapidly to be comprehensible to anyone other than the specialists. Even if federal officials fixed a price or a wage-rate that was correct at time of imposition, changing supply-demand relationships in the market would soon make it inappropriate. In practice, the guideposts prescribed for a particular firm must be inherently arbitrary.

9 Expanding the economic independence and initiative of the enterprise was a pillar of the new economic policy proposed by Premier A. N. Kosygin to the Central Committee of the Communist Party in September 1965. See his "On Improving Industrial Management, Perfecting Planning and Enhancing Economic Incentives in Industrial Production," *Problems of Economics*, Vol. VIII, No. 6 (October 1965).

Guidepost administration is also selective. A few large firms or unions are made the targets for federal action. Many other more culpable organizations escape censure. This selectivity is inequitable, with uneven economic effects. The basic reason why the guideposts broke down in 1966 is that they are not effective operational tools. They do not provide criteria for wage and price determination that are meaningful to private decision-makers.[10]

Recent proposals to revise the guideposts by differentiating the rules governing various industries, or to replace them by an official board to review proposed price and wage changes on an *ad hoc* basis, would not surmount these problems.[11] On the contrary, they would probably destroy what internal logic remains in the present guideposts. They would involve an even larger measure of arbitrary federal tinkering with the market-pricing mechanism, with adverse consequences. For example, if separate productivity guideposts were enforced for each industry, those with the highest productivity gains presumably would be permitted to raise wages more than those with lesser gains. The latter could then suffer from an inadequate supply of labor. Both logic and experience teach that government wage and price

10 This point is made by Professor John T. Dunlop in his paper "Guideposts, Wages and Collective Bargaining," presented to the Conference on Guidepost Policy (Chicago, April 1965).
11 See H. A. Turner and H. Zoeteweij, *Prices, Wages and Incomes Policies* (Geneva, International Labor Office, 1966), p. 105. The Netherlands tried to use productivity measures for individual industries as guides for wage control beginning in 1959 but later abandoned them when it became evident that they were "not amenable to precise administrative control."

controls that are simple enough to be intelligible are inefficient; those that take market complexities into account are inoperable. Comprehensive direct controls are worth their heavy costs only in times of economic mobilization for national defense; these are not our national circumstances today.

Basic Economic Faults of the Guideposts

Serious as are their administrative flaws, the guideposts contain basic economic defects. By attacking the symptoms rather than the causes of cost-push inflation, they divert public and official attention from fundamental remedies. They enable government to escape its responsibilities to impose adequate fiscal and monetary controls of aggregate demand, and to make a *direct* attack on market power and price rigidity. Government officials publicly censure the "irresponsibility" of labor union and business executives, while neglecting their own responsibilities. Although always defended as a supplementary instrument to control inflation, for political reasons the guideposts, in practice, tend to substitute for stern fiscal and monetary restraints. Acrimonious "confrontations" take place between government officials and business and union executives which impair the mutual trust and respect which took so long to develop during the postwar years.

A grave fault of the guideposts is that it weakens the spirit and institutions of a competitive market economy. Federal officials are in the position of telling labor union and business executives that "responsible" behavior consists in *not* drawing the logical inferences from their positions in the markets they confront. Since competitive behavior has been branded "irresponsible," managers are in effect asked to behave non-competitively! What is the true social responsibility of a manager, if not to seek maximum benefits for his organization, in an environment in which his gains are effectively limited by the efforts of others to maximize their gains? If the leaders of our private economy were required to use government guideposts rather than their own long-run self-interests as criteria for decisions, their will and ability to use market guidance could atrophy. This would entail a loss of economic efficiency.

Direct governmental controls are, at heart, a confession of failure of competitive market regulation. They are a retreat from the impersonal market discipline that is the dominant characteristic and greatest source of strength of the U.S. economy. If government discharged *its* basic responsibility for maintaining adequate competition in all markets along with a full-employment level of aggregate demand, the debilitating distinction between "responsible" and competitive behavior would vanish.[12]

Guideposts are also a perverse instrument of economic policy because there is no logical limit to the extension of direct controls, short of placing the economy

12 See *Defense Against Inflation: Policies for Price Stability in a Growing Economy.* (New York, Committee for Economic Development, May 1958), p. 15. Even such a sophisticated group as the Committee for Economic Development appears to have fallen into the error of calling for *both* competition and "voluntary restraint." Adequate competition per se would make "restraint" unnecessary by providing an environment in which private decisions were compatible with the public interests.

in a straitjacket. If wage-rates are to be controlled to limit labor income, how can government defend the freedom of property incomes to rise via larger dividends, rents, and interest payments? The Economic Policy Committee of AFL-CIO has quite logically attacked the guideposts as "an attempt to short-change workers— while there is no effective guideline for prices and no guidelines at all for profits and dividends." [13] Being inherently selective, guideposts produce uneven effects upon the incomes of different economic groups. Once government has embarked upon a policy of direct intervention, there is no logical stopping point short of comprehensive controls.

In order to meet this valid criticism, many European countries have described their programs of direct anti-inflationary control as "incomes policies." [14] Some have sought to apply them to profits and dividends, as well as to wages. However, their observed results do not encourage the U.S. to go down that path. Careful assessment of the operation of "incomes" policies by both American and European economists has produced a concensus that their effectiveness has been limited in extent and duration.[15] They may have suppressed inflation

---

13 Statement of the Economic Policy Committee of AFL-CIO, February 1966. Although one may concur in the cited assertion in this statement, other parts of it, including a willingness to accept "some price inflation," are unacceptable. Labor organizations are likely to oppose proposals made later in this paper to make labor markets more competitive in structure.
14 A brief factual description is given in *Incomes Policies* (Paris, Organization for Economic Cooperation and Development, 1966). Also in H. A. Turner, and H. Zoeteweij, *op. cit.*
15 See H. A. Turner, and H. Zoeteweij, *op. cit.*, p. 144.

for a short time; but underlying pressures of excessive aggregate demand soon asserted themselves. An "incomes" policy in the U.S. would probably be even less effective than it has been in Europe. Our economy is less dependent upon foreign trade and foreign competition. The social concept of "fair shares" commends less support. We have no labor party or government. Our economy is much larger, with a more decentralized organization of labor and system of collective bargaining.[16]

The basic point, however, is that an "incomes" policy is wrong in principle. In a competitive market economy, no factor of production, no economic group, is entitled, by right, to a fixed portion or increment of the real national income. Income shares may be expected to vary over time in accordance with changes in the supply-demand relationships of the factors of production.

The Degree of Incompatibility of Full Employment and Price-Level Stability

To demonstrate the futility of wage-price guideposts is not enough. It still leaves unsolved the problem of reconciling the goal of full employment with a stable price level. Let us first try to measure the dimensions of this problem. How much price inflation does the U.S. economy generate when employment is full? How much unemployment is characteristic of the economy when the price level is stable? It is axiomatic that effective management, of an economy or of an enterprise, calls for a clear

16 See Albert Rees, "An Incomes Policy for the United States," *Journal of Business*, Vol. XXXVIII, No. 4 (October 1965).

definition of goals. Only then can we know when goals have been achieved. Unfortunately, our accepted national goals of "full employment" and a "stable price level" are fuzzy. Not knowing when the economy has reached full employment, there is no agreement on when to end expansionary policies.

The first official U.S. definition of "full employment" was given in the January 1962 *Economic Report* of President Kennedy, which stated: "In the existing economic circumstances, an unemployment rate of about 4 per cent is a reasonable and prudent full employment target for stabilization policy." [17] This working definition expressed the consensus of economists. It recognized that in our huge, technically dynamic, and affluent economy about one in every twenty-five persons in the work force will not be at work even in a time of prosperity for a variety of reasons, such as looking for a first job, changing residence, changing occupation, retraining, or a long lay-off. Four per cent was recognized as an interim full-employment target, to be revised as improvements were made in the structure of the employment market.

The salient question today is whether structural changes in the employment market during the past four years make appropriate an unemployment target ratio substantially under 4 per cent. The January 1966 *Economic Report* answered this question in the affirmative. Yet the evidence it adduced to support its opinion is not convincing, and it did not fix any new full-employment target. While it is true that the education and skills of workers have improved on the average, this apparently

[17] *Economic Report* (January 1966), p. 46. See also p. 8.

has been offset by the higher educational and skill requirements of the jobs that are available. The "automation" of clerical and service as well as manufacturing operations has continued briskly during the past four years, a process reflected in a sustained rise in physical productivity. One is entitled to conclude that full employment is as accurately defined by a 4 per cent unemployment ratio in 1966 as it was in 1962.[18]

The target of a stable price level has usually been defined as *no rise* in the Consumer Price Index. However, this is not a realistic definition. Economic statisticians generally agree that technical procedures in the construction of the CPI give it an upward bias, largely because of tardy recognition of new products and quality improvements.[19] The rise of the CPI from 100.7 during

18 The most satisfactory definition of "full employment" is a condition where the number of job vacancies equals the number of persons seeking work, as Lord Beveridge pointed out in his celebrated report of the 1940s. When this condition obtains, aggregate demand for labor equals aggregate supply, and such unemployment as exists is attributable to the structural problems of matching the skill and locations of vacant jobs with those of unemployed people. The unemployment ratio under conditions of full employment, so defined, will depend upon the structure and functioning of the employment market in a particular economy. Lord Beveridge estimated that full employment in the British economy of the forties meant a three per cent unemployment ratio. Unfortunately, the U.S. lacks comprehensive current data on job vacancies, which makes this definition inoperable.

19 Our "market basket" CPI also has an inflationary bias by ignoring substitutions in consumer purchases of stable-priced for rising-priced items. In a recent study it was concluded that "an annual increase in the (consumer price) index of one per cent or perhaps two per cent might be fully matched by improvements in quality and the availability of new products." See H. A. Turner, and H. Zoeteweij, *op. cit.*, p. 31.

1958 to 108.1 in 1963 indicates that an upward drift of under 1.5 per cent a year was maintained over a six-year period without any tendency toward acceleration.[20] This was, we may infer, really a period of price-level stability. Given present imperfections in the CPI, one may accept an annual rise of around 1.5 per cent a year as being consistent with a stable dollar.

When we define the problem as one of reconciling a 4 per cent unemployment ratio with an annual rise of not over 1.5 per cent in the CPI, it is seen that the task of attaining full employment without real price inflation is more manageable than commonly believed. During the years 1956 and 1957 the employment rate averaged 4.2 and 4.3 per cent. The rise in the CPI was a non-inflationary 1.4 per cent during 1956 and a mildly inflationary 3.5 per cent during 1957. During 1965 an average 4.6 per cent unemployment ratio was associated with a non-inflationary 1.7 per cent rise in the CPI. During the calendar year of 1966, an average unemployment ratio of 3.9 per cent (seasonally adjusted) was accompanied by an annual 3.6 per cent rise in the CPI. These comparisons suggest that a "cost-push" begins only when the unemployment ratio moves within about one-half of a percentage point or 12.5 per cent of the full-employment level. While this marks a regrettable gap between U.S. employment and price-level goals, it is surely not unsuperable.[21]

20 Computed from data in *Economic Indicators* (August 1966).
21 Paul A. Samuelson, and Robert A. Solow, "Analytical Aspects of Anti-Inflation Policy," *American Economic Review*, Vol. 50 (May 1960), pp. 192–94. See also George L. Perry, *Unemployment Money Wage Rates and Inflation* (Cambridge, MIT

*Competitive-Market Policies to Raise the
Employment Ratio without Provoking Inflation*

What public policies would enable the U.S. economy to operate with a 4 per cent unemployment ratio and also maintain a reasonably stable price-level? Clearly, an attack must be made upon the problem of reducing excessive private market power, but this is only one of many measures that are needed.[22] The basic requirements are to speed up the adjustment of the U.S. labor supply to the changing labor requirements of the economy, to limit governmental price-fixing and stabilizing program, and to create an environment in which private wage and price decisions more closely approach those of effective competition. One enters here a neglected and highly controversial area of public policy. However, the major pathways toward a solution are clear enough, and one need make no apology for reminding the reader of their nature.[23]

Press, 1966). Samuelson and Solow reached approximately the same conclusion in 1960 regarding the trade-off relationships between price-level changes and unemployment ratios in the U.S. They estimated 5.5 per cent unemployment with a stable price index, and a 4.5 per cent annual price rise with 3.0 per cent unemployment. Interpolating, 4.0 per cent unemployment would be associated with about a 2 per cent price rise.

22 See Kermit Gordon, *Price-Cost Behavior and Employment Act Objectives* (Washington, The Brookings Institution, Reprint No. 117, 1966), p. 66. Gordon grossly over-simplified the problem by asserting that attainment of U.S. employment and price-level goals would require us "to strip decision makers of market power by breaking up concentrations both in business and labor."

23 Some of these proposals were made by the author in a paper

1 Broaden and enforce the anti-monopoly laws

A first step should be to remove present exemptions and to bring all private economic organizations, including labor unions, cooperatives and professional associations, under the anti-monopoly laws. In principle, *all* private organizations for economic ends should be subject to public scrutiny by the Department of Justice and the courts for monopolistic practices. Such practices include unreasonable restrictions upon entry into trades and professions, and mergers and acquisitions that inhibit competition. The evolution of standards to define "unreasonable" restrictions on entry into a labor union, or extensions of their size that might "tend to create monopoly" would, of course, have to be worked out by the courts on a case-by-case basis as it has been for business firms. Yet the sooner we adopt a *general* anti-monopoly policy, the sooner we shall curb excessive private market power.

The notion that large unions or corporations must be "pulverized" in order to create effective competition is false. The U.S. economy is large enough to tolerate large unions and business firms, provided that the bargaining power on both sides of the tale is not too unequal. In some industries where it is now grossly unequal, a wider application of the principle of creating countervailing

---

submitted to the Joint Economic Committee of Congress in 1958. See "Maintaining Prosperity without Inflation: Objectives, Problems, and Policies," *The Relationship of Prices to Economic Stability and Growth.* Compendium published by the Joint Economic Committee (Washington, U.S. Govt. Printing Office, March 31, 1958), pp. 647–49.

bargaining power on the side of management probably would be desirable. Without exploring here all of the complex issues, it is clear that a first step must be a *general* application of anti-monopoly laws.

2 *Lower barriers to foreign trade and widen the area of competition*

Perhaps the most important constraint upon the rise of wage-rates and prices in the American steel industry during recent years has been the competition of foreign steel. The wage demands of steel union leaders have been moderated by the knowledge that jobs would be curtailed by over-aggressive behavior. Managements of steel firms have been much tougher bargainers, knowing that increases in unit costs could not readily be passed on to customers. These comments apply with equal force to the textile, automotive, and other industries. Foreign trade widens the area of competition. It tends to make wage and price decisions conform to the competitive norm. U.S. foreign trade policy should give conscious recognition to its effects upon domestic competition. Priority should be given to the lowering of barriers to imports competing with products of those industries where domestic business or union market power needs taming. Trade liberalization is, of course, desirable on many other grounds.

3 *Accelerate worker retraining and relocation programs*

Few spending programs should have a higher priority in the federal budget than those intended to reduce the present mismatch between the labor skills demanded by a technically advancing economy and those possessed by the work force. This is especially true of programs that will advance the general education and vocational skills of youths and minority groups, where the unemployment ratios are always highest. A bold beginning has been made in the Manpower Retraining Act, the Area Development Act, the Education Act, and other programs of recent years. The difficulty is that automation has been changing the demand for labor as fast as these programs have altered the supply. The answer must be to speed up and expand these programs, and to invent new ways to accelerate labor supply adjustments. Apprenticeship, vocational education, and on-the-job-training programs are promising methods. By all these means a substantial reduction can be made in structural unemployment.

4 Gradually withdraw from governmental price-fixing and price-supporting activities

One reason for the downward inflexibility of the price-level and its tendency to creep upward even in the face of unemployment is numerous federal programs for fixing or supporting prices in agriculture, petroleum, basic metals, and other commodities. In fact, the federal government is by far the most important agent in "administered" prices. The federal farm price support programs help to boost the price of food, which has about a 25 per cent weighting in the CPI. The restrictive quota on crude oil imports now raises the cost of petroleum to the U.S. refiner more than 50 per cent. Stockpiling programs for aluminum, zinc, lead, copper, and other metals are administered ostensibly in the interests of national security, but have also acquired strong price stabilizing overtones. An orderly withdrawal from all federal price-supporting activities would restore downward flexibility to many important prices. It would help take some of the upward "creep" out of the CPI. It would make the achievement of our employment target under a stable price level much easier. An extra dividend of such a withdrawal would be the greater economic efficiency attained by allowing prices to perform their resource-allocating function.

5 Defer increases and extensions of coverage of the minimum wage

Minimum wage laws are really a special case of government price fixing. Congress has recently approved increases in the minimum wage from $1.25 per hour to $1.60 per hour over a two-year period, and expansion of its coverage to trades employing eight millions of additional workers. It is difficult to conceive of legislation more damaging to our nation's quest for full employment without inflation. The differential between the pay of skilled and unskilled workers has gotten out of equilibrium in recent years. Unskilled labor is now relatively overpriced, and there has been a strong upward drift in the ratio of the minimum wage to the average wage.[24] The broad result of substantial increases in the minimum wage has been to curtail job opportunities for less skilled workers—primarily youths and those in minority groups, whose productivity is relatively low. Raising the mini-

24 See Arthur F. Burns, *The Management of Prosperity* (New York, Columbia University Press, 1966).

mum wage puts pressure on businessmen to install labor-saving machinery and to let unskilled workers go—at a time when the U.S. economy has a surplus of unskilled labor and a capital shortage! Although it is defended as a measure to improve the incomes of poor people, a higher minimum wage has the effect of condemning many of them to permanent unemployment. Moreover, it tends to generate a certain amount of cost-push among unions whose members work for wages close to the legal minimum. Thus, it may add several tenths of a percentage point to the unemployment ratio. It is, indeed, a policy to create unemployment.[25] At the least, the application of the higher minimum wage to youths should be suspended.

6 Expand research into labor markets and improve their functioning

Despite their crucial importance, firm knowledge of the structure and functioning of U.S. labor markets is seriously deficient. We lack an adequate basis for public policy decisions. The amount and temporal variation of job vacancies, the amount and effects of overtime work and second-job holding, methods of reducing seasonal variations in employment, and ways to enable employees to adjust to technological and locational changes of employment are among the subjects that urgently need attention. Long-term forecasts of the growth of the U.S. economy and its several sectors and industries need to

25 Mechanization that is forced by governmental wage-fixing imposes large social costs. See Yale Brozen, and Milton Friedman, *The Minimum Wage—Who Pays?* (Washington, The Free Society Association, Inc., April 1966).

be translated into forecasts of demand for labor skills of various kinds, so that youths may be trained and directed into the fields of greatest opportunity. The U.S. Department of Labor needs funds and staff to get the answers, which can help make the U.S. job market more fluid and flexible.[26]

The Matter of Timing

Critics of competitive-market policies to increase the employment ratio without provoking inflation may agree with its substance, but object to the long time required to produce structural solutions. They ask whether it is not better, in the interim, to continue to apply expansionary fiscal-monetary measures and to accept the price inflation that comes with full employment. Will not the economy sacrifice obtainable growth if aggregate demand is held to non-inflationary levels?

It should be pointed out, in response, that much of the "growth" in monetary demand during a period of general price inflation is in the price level and not in the real supply of goods and services. It is "money illusion." More important is the consideration that price inflation

26 It has been suggested that the size of negotiated wage increases might be reduced by offering unions (a) long-term contracts incorporating annual productivity "improvement" factors, or (b) worker participation in enterprise profits. These are not promising measures. Because the increase in labor productivity in an enterprise cannot be predicted in advance, a wage agreement predicated upon specified future increases in productivity throws a risk on the firm that could have adverse effects upon its investment and employment. While there is much to be said in favor of wider profit-sharing with workers, American unions have not generally favored it.

reduces the rise in productivity which is the most important source of growth in real output. Monetary-fiscal
measures to curb inflation may create some unemployment, particularly of employees of little experience or
low productivity who are drawn into jobs in a tight labor
market. Yet the loss of real output from their disem-
ployment is likely to be more than offset over a period
of time by the extra productivity resulting from the
maintenance of a stable price level. In a regime of stable
prices, workers have stronger reasons to hold their jobs
and work efficiently, and managers have more powerful
incentives to reduce costs and use capital effectively.
The adverse effects of inflation upon productivity is a
relationship well established by statistical analysis as
well as logic.

Monetary-fiscal checks upon aggregate demand thus
serve to maintain the secular rise in productivity and to
prevent its deterioration. Far from calling for sacrifices
in real economic growth upon an altar of price-level
stability, as inflationists contend, they contribute to the
goals of rapid growth and balance in international payments.

Conclusions

The principal conclusions of this analysis may now
be stated briefly. Wage-price guideposts were proposed
in 1962 to help prevent "cost-push" inflation from beginning before full employment was attained in the U.S.
economy. When used only as a means of educating the
public in wage-price-productivity relationships, the guide-

posts can play a limited but useful role. When used as a system of federally-enforced wage and price controls—as was increasingly the case after 1964—the guideposts were detrimental to the economy. Being ineffective substitutes for adequate fiscal and monetary controls, they led economic policy down a dead-end street. Present guideposts are incapable of equitable and efficient federal administration; and there is no way to revise them into operationally useful tools of policy.

The basic means of reconciling full employment with a stable price level is to restore effective competition in all sectors of the U.S. economy. This requires governmental measures to enforce the anti-monopoly laws against labor unions as well as business firms, to widen the area of competition by opening up more domestic markets to foreign trade, to reduce federal price-fixing and stabilizing activities, including minimum wage legislation, and to expand research designed to make U.S. employment markets function more effectively. A competitive-market approach to the problem that the guideposts failed to solve will require time. Yet, the dimensions of the problem are not so large, and the manifold gains from its solution are so great that one is justified in believing that our nation can achieve a timely resolution.